HOW SWEET THE SOUND

CAROLE BOSTON WEATHERFORD • ILLUSTRATED BY FRANK MORRISON

The Story of Amazing Grace

A ATHENEUM BOOKS FOR YOUNG READERS   New York • London • Toronto • Sydney • New Delhi

Slave ship *Greyhound*, ocean faring;
Young John, homeward, brawling, swearing.

Fierce storm, sea squall, ripping sails;
Young John wakes to crewmen's wails.

Fearing this night is his last,
Trembling, John relives his past:

Mother teaching hymns of praise;
Little angel, John obeys.

Bible study, growing wise;
Lessons end when Mother dies.

Father—captain—
John to sea;
No more prayers
on bended knee.

Scoundrel, rascal, picking fights;
Fussing, fuming, never right.

John meets Mary, bloom so sweet;
Pitter-patter, heart skips beat.

Navy nabs him, John jumps ship;
Lovesick, captured, beaten, whipped.

Slaver's servant, bound in chains;
Meals of raw fish, belly pains.

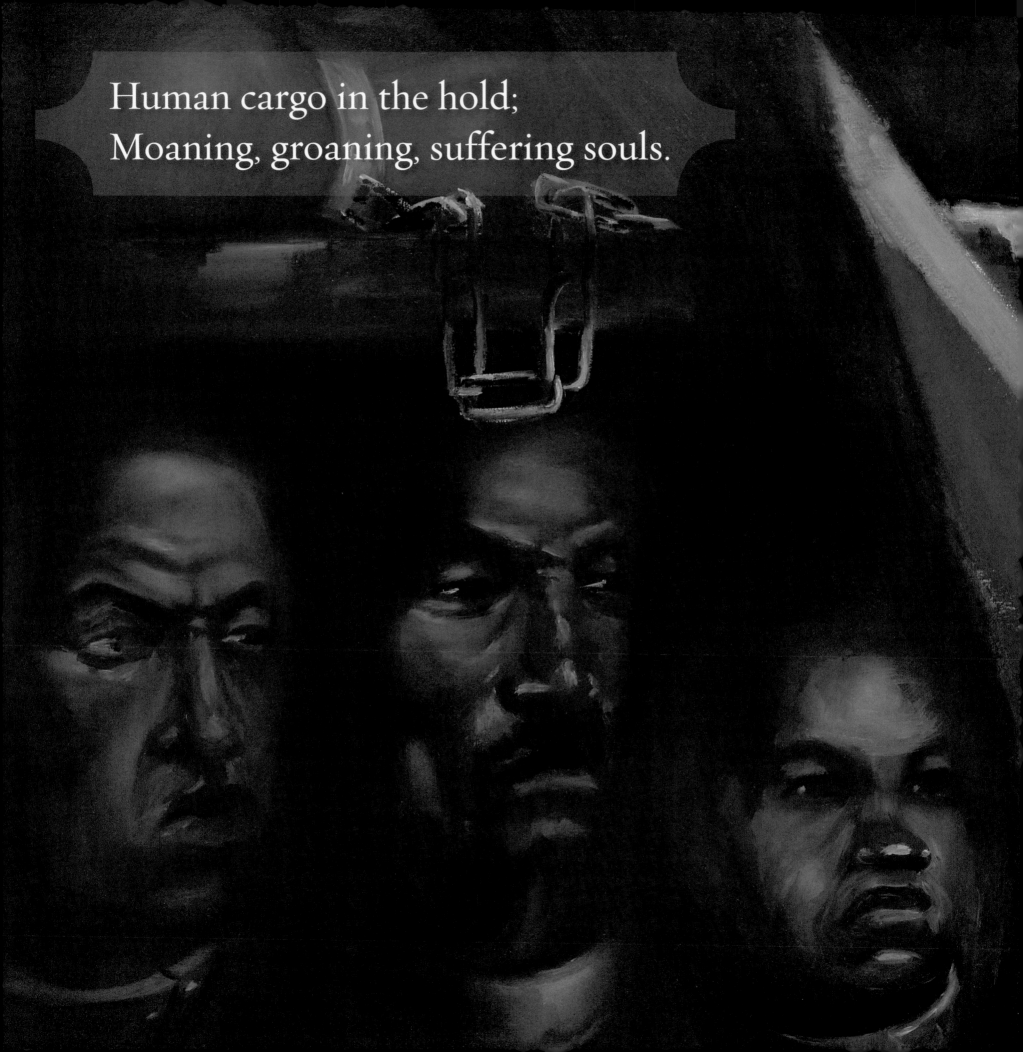

Human cargo in the hold;
Moaning, groaning, suffering souls.

Wasted life, now gale wind–tossed;
Young John fears that all is lost.

Pumping water, John plugs leaks.
Raging storm makes sea dogs weak.

Captain shouts, "John, steer the ship!"
Ten long hours the helm he grips.

Praying, pleading off and on,
"Lord, just let me see the dawn."

Peaceful ocean, lifting fog.
Greyhound drifting, waterlogged.

Crew bails water day and night;
Rations thinning, bite by bite.

Island spotted, over there!
Eyes deceive in high-noon glare.

Hope of reaching England sinks.
Crew brands John a Jonah, jinx.

Crew taunts, "Dump him overboard!"
John spared only by the Lord.

Greyhound tugged by unseen hand,
Crew at long last glimpses land.

Safe at home, brought through the storm,
Young John Newton is reborn.

Trusting God as compass, guide,
John is captain; Mary, bride.

After John retires from sea,
He preaches to end slavery.

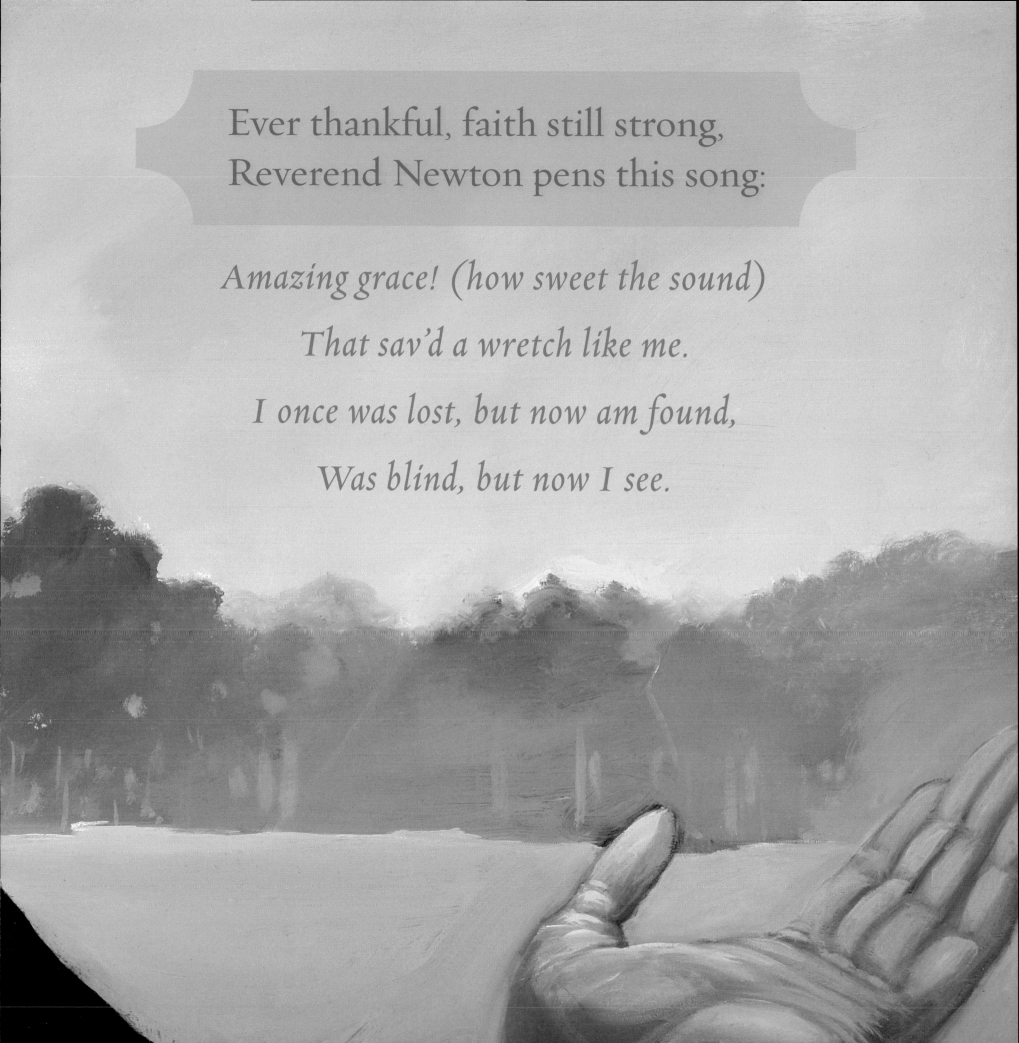

Ever thankful, faith still strong,
Reverend Newton pens this song:

Amazing grace! (how sweet the sound)

That sav'd a wretch like me.

I once was lost, but now am found,

Was blind, but now I see.

Lyrics sail across the sea,
Meet a folksy melody.

Shape-note singers sound it plain.
All aboard the gospel train!

Cherokees, a westbound band,
Driven from their eastern lands.

Trudging on the Trail of Tears,
They chant this song to draw God near.

Cannon fire, battlefield.
Weary soldiers, bloodied, kneel.

Hymn, a comfort to the corps
In the throes of Civil War.

Choirs make the song their own.
Newton's timeless hymn has grown.

Verses added here and there
Till this song is like a prayer.

On records and on radio,
Stirring words that millions know.

Mahalia, oh, how sweet *her* sound!
Hymn that's hummed the whole world round.

Praising God in each translation.
A leader sings to heal a nation.

Call to conscience, plea for peace,
Hymn whose wonders never cease.

Amazing Grace

Amazing grace! (how sweet the sound)
That sav'd a wretch like me.
I once was lost, but now am found,
Was blind, but now I see.

'Twas grace that taught my heart to fear,
And grace my fears reliev'd;
How precious did that grace appear,
The hour I first believ'd!

Thro' many dangers, toils and snares,
I have already come;
'Tis grace hath brought me safe thus far,
And grace will lead me home.

The Lord has promis'd good to me,
His word my hope secures;
He will my shield and portion be,
As long as life endures.

Yes, when this flesh and heart shall fail,
And mortal life shall cease;
I shall possess, within the veil,
A life of joy and peace.

The earth shall soon dissolve like snow,
The sun forbear to shine;
But God, who call'd me here below,
Will be forever mine.

When we've been there ten thousand years,
Bright shining as the sun,
We've no less days to sing God's praise
Than when we'd first begun.*

*See author's note

Author's Note

The popular hymn "Amazing Grace" recounts the stormy night when hymn writer John Newton opened his heart to God. John was born in 1725 in London, England. His mother, who taught him Scripture and hymns, died when he was seven. Thus, John spent part of his childhood at sea with his father, a captain. As a teen, John was pressed into service by the Royal Navy and was nearly starved while working as a servant to a slave trader in Africa. These experiences hardened his heart. John drank, cursed, and fought. Even the meanest sailors feared him.

In March 1748, Newton was a passenger on the slave ship *Greyhound* when a violent storm struck. Fearing death, Newton turned to God. Amazingly, the battered ship weathered the storm. Grateful that God had spared his life, Newton gradually changed his ways. He studied the Bible and married his childhood sweetheart, Mary. However, he also captained his own slave ship. After an illness forced him to give up seafaring, he worked as a surveyor of tides. But he felt called to be a minister.

In 1764, Newton began pastoring a church in Olney, England. With poet William Cowper, Newton wrote hymns for weekly prayer meetings. Over time, he changed his views about human bondage and raised his pen against slavery. His "Thoughts upon the African Slave Trade" helped bring slavery to an end in the British Empire.

By 1779, Newton had written 280 hymns. He died in 1807 in London, England.

In the years that followed, British colonists brought the hymn with them to North America. There, the lyrics were paired with a folk tune known as "New Britain." Shape-note singers, who sang a cappella, popularized the song at camp meetings. Over time, verses were added to the original hymn. For example, African Americans attached lyrics that spoke to their struggle. The hymn was sung by Cherokees—in their mother tongue—on the Trail of Tears, a forced migration from their native lands in the East to territory west of the Mississippi. Civil War soldiers; African Americans during slavery, segregation, and the civil rights movement; and anti-war protestors during the Vietnam War leaned on Newton's lyrics. President Barack Obama even led the congregation in singing the hymn at a funeral of a church-shooting victim. Many renditions of the hymn have been recorded, by artists ranging from gospel singer Mahalia Jackson and folk singer Judy Collins to rock and roll legend Elvis Presley. The lyrics used in this book are likely from the earliest published version of the hymn and can be found at anointedlinks.com/amazing_grace, with the exception of the last verse, which Harriet Beecher Stowe wrote for *Uncle Tom's Cabin*. Translated into many languages, "Amazing Grace" continues to inspire the world over.

Further Reading, Listening, and Viewing

Granfield, Linda. Illustrated by Janet Wilson. *Out of Slavery: The Journey to Amazing Grace*. Tundra, 2009.

Granfield, Linda. Illustrated by Janet Wilson. *Amazing Grace: The Story of the Hymn*. Tundra, 1997.

Howat, Irene. *John Newton: A Slave Set Free*. CF4Kids, 2002.

Turner, Steve. *Amazing Grace: The Story of America's Most Beloved Song*, HarperCollins, 2002.

Bill Moyers: Amazing Grace, PBS 1990. billmoyers.com/content/amazing-grace-bill-moyers

Amazing Grace Collection, Library of Congress. memory.loc.gov/diglib/ihas/html/grace/grace-home.html

Cowper and Newton Museum, Olney, England. cowperandnewtonmuseum.org.uk

Many wonderful performances of "Amazing Grace" can be seen on YouTube, including versions by these artists:

Mahalia Jackson

Judy Collins

Aretha Franklin

BeBe Winans

Elvis Presley

Barack Obama

John Legend

Soweto Gospel Choir

For my amazingly gracious mother, Carolyn W. Boston
—C. B. W.

For my Sunday school teacher Mrs. Sanders—thanks for sharing your wisdom
—F. M.

atheneum

ATHENEUM BOOKS FOR YOUNG READERS
An imprint of Simon & Schuster Children's Publishing Division
1230 Avenue of the Americas, New York, New York 10020
Text copyright © 2018 by Carole Boston Weatherford
Illustrations copyright © 2018 by Frank Morrison
All rights reserved, including the right of reproduction in whole or in part in any form.
ATHENEUM BOOKS FOR YOUNG READERS is a registered trademark of Simon & Schuster, Inc. Atheneum logo is a trademark of Simon & Schuster, Inc.
For information about special discounts for bulk purchases, please contact Simon & Schuster Special Sales at 1-866-506-1949 or business@simonandschuster.com.
The Simon & Schuster Speakers Bureau can bring authors to your live event. For more information or to book an event, contact the Simon & Schuster Speakers Bureau at 1-866-248-3049 or visit our website at www.simonspeakers.com.
Book design by Ann Bobco
The text for this book was set in Requiem.
The illustrations for this book were rendered in oil on canvas and illustration board.
Manufactured in China • 0218 SCP
First Edition
10 9 8 7 6 5 4 3 2 1
Library of Congress Cataloging-in-Publication Data
Names: Weatherford, Carole Boston, 1956- author. | Morrison, Frank, 1971- illustrator.
Title: How sweet the sound : the story of Amazing grace / Carole Boston Weatherford ; illustrated by Frank Morrison.
Description: New York : Atheneum Books for Young Readers, [2018]
Identifiers: LCCN 2017003372
ISBN 9781481472067 (hardcover)
ISBN 9781481472074 (eBook)
Subjects: LCSH: Newton, John, 1725-1807—Juvenile literature. | Amazing grace (Hymn)—Juvenile literature. | Hymn writers—England—Biography—Juvenile literature.
Classification: LCC BV330.N48 W43 2018 Y DDC 264/.23—dc23
LC record available at https://lccn.loc.gov/2017003372